The Painting-Room

Poetry by the same author

COLLECTIONS

The Rain-Giver
The Dream-House
Time's Oriel
Waterslain

SELECTION

Between My Father and My Son

LIMITED EDITIONS

On Approval
My Son
Alderney: The Nunnery
Norfolk Poems (with John Hedgecoe)
More than I am (with Ralph Steadman)
Petal and Stone
Above the Spring Line (with Malte Sartorius)
The Wanderer (with James Dodds)
The Seafarer (with Inger Lawrence)
Oenone in January (with John Lawrence)

TRANSLATIONS

The Battle of Maldon and Other Old English Poems
Beowulf
The Exeter Book Riddles
The Anglo-Saxon World

EDITOR

Running to Paradise: An Introductory Selection of the Poems of
    W. B. Yeats
Poetry 2 (Arts Council – with Patricia Beer)
The Oxford Book of Travel Verse

The Painting-Room

and other poems

Kevin Crossley-Holland

Hutchinson

London Melbourne Auckland Johannesburg

© Kevin Crossley-Holland 1988
All rights reserved
First published in 1988 by
Hutchinson & Co. (Publishers) Ltd

An imprint of Century Hutchinson Limited

Brookmount House, 62–65 Chandos Place, London WC2N 4NW

Hutchinson Publishing Group (Australia) Pty Ltd
16–22 Church Street, Hawthorn, Melbourne, Victoria 3122

Hutchinson Group (NZ) Ltd
32–34 View Road, PO Box 40-086, Glenfield, Auckland 10

Hutchinson Group (SA) Pty Ltd
PO Box 337, Bergvlei 2012, South Africa

© Kevin Crossley-Holland 1988

Set in Linotron Bembo by
Rowland Phototypesetting Ltd, Bury St Edmunds, Suffolk

Printed and bound in Great Britain by
Anchor Brendon Ltd, Tiptree, Essex

ISBN 0 9173489 4

for Gillian, my wife

Acknowledgements

Poems in this book have first appeared in *Antaeus*, *P N Review*, *The Poetry Review*, *Z L R*, *Poetry Book Society Anthology 1987*, *The Times Literary Supplement* and *Poetry Wales*

'The Painting-Room' was commissioned by Anglia Television and formed part of their celebration of John Constable transmitted on *Folio* on 25th February, 1988.

'In The Garden Tent' was commissioned by the Tate Gallery and printed in *With a Poet's Eye* (Tate Gallery Publications).

'Above the Spring Line' was commissioned by the Francis Kyle Gallery and published in a limited edition with an etching by Malte Sartorius.

'Oenone in January' was first published in a limited edition, with engravings by John Lawrence, by the Old Stile Press.

Contents

THE
PAINTING-ROOM

During his French lessons a long pause would frequently occur, which his master would be the first to break, saying, 'Go on, I am not asleep: Oh! now I see you are in your painting-room.'

– C. R. Leslie

1 The Happiest Hours

That scamp! Elbows and buttocks up,
palms pressed to the juices.
Look at his mop of Saxon hair!

Where he has stared at life
in spawn, still half-asleep,
and netted newts,
and cupped a palpitating frog,
he trains his whole body
and, careless, quenches his thirst again.

Doesn't he know? Has no one said?
Think of poor Lily and Maud,
third and fourth of ten.
They drank stagnant water and
died in the morning.

And what of those dangers
he knows almost nothing of:
the madcaps and skiwanken; victims
turned destroyers; shallow graves.

Now he's turning this way.
I could quite easily catch him up
and, like a lover, hold him to me
redeemed.

When my own daughters sing,
when they hop about
like parched peas on a drumhead,
the weight of the whole world lightens.

Sometimes I could do away with adults,
all their conditions and affectations.
I respect children
who flatter nobody.

Each stroke as the first stroke:
unconfused.
Each word as the first word: exhilarant.

I'll look again.
Half my life is looking
to find myself once more and young.

2 Every Stile and Stump

This is the path I'll take today.

This is the stile
where once and only once
I found white violets
that straddles the path I'll take today.

And this is the stump of a pollarded willow:
it gave six poles to build the stile
where once and only once
I found white violets
that straddles the path I'll take today.

3 Creatures of a Landscape

The truant with his rod,
and cap on the back of his head;
the apple-face on the passing lighter;
and the lad astride the carthorse,
yoked to his destiny:

I'm looking at
the creatures of a paradise garden
they will never leave entirely.

How little will happen
in the whole span of their lives
not already present and planted.
They're almost fixed!

For them as for you and me
the ethic of work
will not be a matter of choice
or self-discovery
but almost an inheritance:
a fierce imperative decreed over their cradles
by a stern godmother.

And when we believe
that whatsoever we do or say
has moral implications,
it's only what our parents told us
and we observe each day
in the order of this land around us.

This dear, familiar, unshowy Eden!
It's the child of history.
It feeds me and I'll nourish it.

4   The Language of Light

I rise with the rising bell
every day of the week.
The river is my pointer
to read the landscape's book.

I'll sit and watch these willow
leaves silvered by the wind
until they are impressed
on the cool page of my mind.

And then these twisted roots
dressed with wads of sponge:
I'll watch them in this calm sun
until the shadows change.

I'll live in these meadows
and trace each variant.
It's with their light they speak
the language of the heart.

5 Correspondences

That's her!
So well disposed to the world:
the gaze unstopped, the kind shoulder.

But on my way here
I saw her in the cornfield:
her carriage, her smouldering mane.
She was gathering with the gleaners.

And that grave girl by the porch:
when I heard her,
soft and foggy
as a flute at the bottom of its register,
I thought for a moment . . .

She surprises me
everywhere
and I say to myself
there is no time when I have not loved her.

I can hear my own voice.
Not proving signs or symbols
but correspondences
are what I'm looking for.

As I walk with the river
and hear, or think I hear,
the far, late harvest bell,
I see her
in the sweet incline of this willow,
the moist leaves. The dry whispers
of the flags are like a Greek chorus.

And here, this torso, aching and arched . . .

Ox-bow and lock and race:
there's laughter in the water
and salt in her veins . . .

That's her!
Did you see her
invested
and trailing green-and-gold chains?

6 Like Light that Gilds

She loves me and her love is light
like light that gilds the river's braid,
when water-meadows drown in shade
and Bergholt's wrapped in rings of night.

Her guardians check, forbid and blight
and still her colours do not fade.
She loves me and her love is light
like light that gilds the river's braid.

Do they believe she has no fight?
Or think our love can be betrayed?
Shining, constant and unafraid,
she guides my hand and gilds my sight

like light that gilds the river's braid.

7 *Quiet and Unquiet*

In the lap of water
and the company of watermen:

the boatwright with peaceful hands
building the lighter
that will lift with the lock
the keeper is turning;
and the poler, all purpose and clout,
about to yell
at the fisherman dibbling for nothing much.

There is something
similar about these well–tempered men:
their calm brows and their bearing
and every line of their bodies
announce a complete want of anxiety.

As if to advertise the manual life,
or to say
the rod assuages,
or to commend the properties of water.

When I grow quiet,
and ready myself, and start to write,
I am one
of this engaged and placid company.

It's off the page and outside the frame
my mind snags.

Errant son, or telephone silent,
time short and money short:
the shadows lengthen,
everywhere the causes of indisposition.
It was the same for you.

Fisher was right:
worry hurts the stomach more than arsenic.
It soon generates nothing but itself.

And yet to celebrate
this company of watermen
at their usual stations, calm and accepting . . .

I think we would agree
the presence of unquiet
in some small measure quite essential,
vital as yeast.

8 Oak Leaf

This little gossip, silly
and still crumpled, tender
as a tongue! This lobe's twice
pierced, this mole almost amber . . .
      this one and this one

I picked it from the sapling
you planted at the gate,
now ample as a cumulus
childbearing and forthright
      this one and this one
      and the world is wide

No two hours are alike
and no two leaves on a tree,
Let me learn the singular
green lessons of the eye
      this one and this one
      and the world is wide
      this one and only

9 *In Pursuit*

Under rookwings
and the tatty crown,
under the lanes of clouds,
dove and lily and oyster in the dome,
the labours of the months proceed:

the ferryman and his mate
and the blinkered white horse in harness,
the plough, the little boat
with its nose in shadow, its oars
at this moment shipped,

all part of the same arduous story
the water reflects
and invigorates.

Observation close and continual . . .
to realize, not to feign . . .
less to inspire than inform . . .
and this pursuit
not to be looked on with blind wonder
but legitimate, scientific and mechanical.

I understand this too:
matter is deadweight
and form nothing but a shape
the breath of life makes beautiful.

Lightness and brightness.
The tint of English daylight, cool.

When Chantrey took your palette
and scumbled the whole foreground
with smears of asphaltum:
'There goes all my dew.'

10   In My Painting-Room

Wherever I step wherever I look
the canvas-weave is covered in blossom,
impasted with chestnut, cherry and lilac,

Queen Anne's lace and ropes of laburnum.
My galloping boys spring out of the brush;
and my girls, all gingham and sweet alyssum,

skip past the millrace's passion-and-rush;
and now my wife glances up at our home –
I'll dress her in sunlight: a loop of gold wash.

Child-willow, cloud-woman, the river's in bloom:
surge and reflection – life, resurrection –
lift their bright voices in my painting-room.

In The Garden Tent

What rhymes with aeolian chimes, swaying guardian
   trees?
Home sweet home, between-times, afternoons at ease.

What rhymes with this turquoise-striped, faded
   awning?
The sagging oak-canopy, the shaded nave yawning.

Two girls in crinoline: haircomb, bustle, stay?
White water gliding, the trill of light at play.

And, in their hands, *Persuasion*? 'The Lady of Shalott'?
Am I locked in a dream and is time running out?

Then the snake Doubt advances, hissing 'yes and yes'.
The perfect rhymes canker in Churchyard's paradise.

A *Note on* The White House at Chelsea

Girtin's gleam is your own house
the one you lived in as a boy
and have not seen for so many years

or is it that still–empty room
the lance of sunlight will pierce
giving tongue to each dancing speck

the dark waters chuckle and pull
you to pieces it is yesterday
it is your luminous tomorrow

Truths and Evasions

('Dreams of a Summer Night – Scandinavian Painting
   at the Turn of the Century', Hayward Gallery, 1986)

And stones at the water's edge
which by immersion
not by moving
learn the water

*

blue upon blue upon blue upon blue

*

white faces girls' faces
floating up out of darkness

*

one prepares to leave school
one blows a cuckoo clock
one stares up from sewing

*

the cherry lips the full mouth
of the midnight dancer
already the reaper
is treading towards her hut

*

composed grave women who knew
for one midsummer night
their wombs contained
(the illusion of) an answer

*

world-without-end light
light from within

*

inside you is a dwarf
inside you a giant
the gods were tragedians

*

standing apart on the balcony
and seeing that skiff
and that clump of reeds
over the water a mile off
so much more sharply than each other

★

little said or nothing said
as if one were unlikely
to reach any understanding
by the way of words

★

the long sleeves the long dresses
the long hair
the night

Making a Rainbow

The children are making a rainbow

The children of Sling and Stroat
sons and daughters of the freeminers
have forgotten the scowls
they have lifted their eyes
they are all making a rainbow

Richard of York says Miss Rose
Richard of York gave battle in vain
and on the other side
of the hardboard partition
Miss Nicholas writes Roygbiv
in a cursive hand
and then on the blackboard in capitals
ROYGBIV

Red as rose petals, a whole poppy field,
embarrassment, the blood of a god . . .

Orange though is ugsome
all entrails and ventricles
the best of it
carrot juice and *food Thor spat out*

The tears of the sun,
a green sky-serpent . . .

Blue says Miss Nicholas says Miss Rose
on the other side of the hardboard partition
blue is blue is
the Blue Bird of Happiness

Now *the shell of a wood-louse,*
a basket of Victoria plums:
indigo is more sheen than substance

And violet last is flow and greeting
ocean's curtsy, seacoal burning,
a sky-wave like the rainbow herself

All in all one tiny girl raises
an ice-mirror to reflect the sun
and a boy begins *The first rainbow*
was made by men living before 989 . . .
Neither of these extremists
wins much sympathy

The sweet rain ceases
the sun goes in

It is in the sky
says an earnest joker
(a *sage enfant* from the Pludds)
because if it was on the ground
you wouldn't be able to see it
and there wouldn't be any point
in having it

It is in the word
thinks Miss Nicholas thinks Miss Rose
in the word
sons and daughters rainbow children

Emmeringer Hölzel

for Susanne Lugert

If you say light
I say
    what kind of light
if green
    what kind of green
           ★
in sunlight
water streams over stone
    (sound above silence)
and I note
        scan
        smithereens of quicksilver
        glitter of tines
           ★
the virulence of weed
underwater
        broken chancel
of leaves girlish and chrysoprase
the river gives back
           and the gloom
under the bridge
        loden
          ★
the way you talk is green
              is light
pouring through one another
that moment
        in the sunlight
they cannot be divided
         ★

how the float bobs and dances
each stipule and petiole
                              each cipher
on the surface
                    how the syllables wink
all your life and all my life
up on this bridge wordfishing

Sounds

for my father on his seventieth birthday

You dug the chalky soil; we blazed spring-trails
through high, sopping beechwoods; and in the shed
examined, catalogued and then displayed
quartz crystals, coins, potsherds from Bledlow Ridge,
fossils from the chalk-pit; at night I heard
you play – while you charmed babeldom I slept.

After a while I brought you drafts. I thought
the gardener and walker-in-the-rain,
the patient keeper with whom once I found
a Constantine, the music-man whose Dance
was sung in mildewed church, cathedral nave
and concert hall would know about word-spells.

You treated them with proper seriousness.
I see you at your study door, smiling,
taking the sheets; and then you close your eyes,
withdraw into that magic gloom of books,
piano, harmonisphere, preparing for
our sessions with small signs and spider-marks.

You thinned my words like seedlings. *And avoid
long words where short suffice.* (Work; will do.)
For vogue and buzz and all-too-commonplace
you wrote in almost timeless substitutes
(ex-Yeats, ex-Graves). *Revise and then revise.
Our second thoughts strike deeper than the first.*

Sometimes you mused aloud, or asked me how
my craft related to the science of sound –
abstract in this, its power akin to music.
And sound, you told me then, *includes silence.*
One part of the performance, integral . . .
I hear myself. Hear all that's left unsaid.

Naming You

We have not snared you
with the net of a name
we have not tamed you

you are energy the one
word that is every word
the sound of the gong

come into the garden
and we will sing you
white stars green leaves

such spring-fever
the birds hop and cheep
around your sleepy head

the surge and shining
the rocking of tall trees
in the eager wind

who are you what are you
but the little sister
of this world around you

morning star and sparrow
bluebell smouldering
the attentive yew

*

but the dance of time
the argument of choice
fingers reach out

well the world can wait
we are disciples
and nothing is arbitrary

you are your own word
and cannot grow out of
a careless visitation

you declare yourself
smiling bubble-blower
your eyes gentian blue

lolling by the willow
your bald head askew
like a medieval saint

come home little sister
take your proper place
in this shining garden

dear daughter come home
come home we are here
and listening for your name

Swaddlings

When you say soft

I unwrap the last veil
of mist
with my fingertips

touch the gauze
red gold
spread across the face
of her sleeping sister

drowse in the house
swaddled in rain
I cannot see
cannot hear

and not even these
are soft

as her innocent skin

Oenone in January

January 1st: Beginning

Fingers chapped, the clean year picked and scraped
to a glint. Halley's Comet a milk burr.
Over the long field silhouettes, guffaws,
resolutions. Then the boisterous wind.

January 2nd: Ages

She carts, cherishes and upbraids her dolls,
sowing the seeds of her own motherhood.
She is every age already. You look
as she sleeps: creaseless ancient Infanta.

January 3rd: Pretence

You core it and she eats the skin, the flesh
and then the hole! When she covers her eyes
she is hidden. She deceives you with pearls.
You hear her laughter in the swollen stream.

January 4th: Taming

Buttons, clips, pins – she always takes her tithe.
She drills tins and bottles. Nothing counter
passes without some question or comment.
This fierce attempt on the unwieldy world!

January 5th: Absences

Not maybes – those tassels whiskers, that lump
in the mattress tigerish – but maybe nots:
Can't see them! Can't hear them! Am I alone?
Bawling existentialist before dawn.

January 6th: Animateur

Spangles on her pane. Icicles wrist-thick,
thick as ropes and candid. Dark clots knitted
up in the elms. The whole frieze in need of
its *animateur*. She opens one eye.

January 7th: Imagining

You smile, murmur *mouse*, think she clambers up
to share one pillow and rehearse the day . . .
Gulls circle mewing. You turn to the clock,
and it's not even time for her to wake.

January 8th: Invocation

All morning the sleet slanted in. She stripped
to the waist and donned seven necklaces.
Doily, felt-tips (heavy duty): she raised
a rose garden and entered it, singing.

January 9th: Numbers

One more, no more . . . In her reckoning, what
is ever quite complete? *Where has he went?*
It's a shame they can't come both. I am three
years old; when will I be all the numbers?

January 10th: Hair

A thousand clefs of curls. Her mother laughs
and says *corn-gold* (her own is titian).
Bright cloud, you think; grace notes of the skylark,
ocean, elixir . . . *Nope*, she says. *Ginger!*

January 11th: Half-Brother

She knows it's almost time for him to go.
Silver chatterbox, she trots at his heels,
dragoons him into last loud games. He smiles,
devoted, tolerant; a kind of god.

January 12th: Recognition

Good morning path! Oh! good morning puddle!
Blithe bubble all the way to Sunday School.
St Francis' sister, greeting one and all
as newborn and equal and integral.

January 13th: Rites

She takes your lobes between fingers and thumbs,
gently massages; rubs noses; warbles
into one ear. Close your eyes. Celebrate
the siren rites of the true Daughterhood!

January 14th: Rivals

Each used to undivided attention;
each queering the other's pitch. Carnations
blaze in the razor sunlight. Two *divas*
(old and young) glaring across their breakfasts!

January 15th: Chastening

That weal on the back of her hand your hand
inflicted, and the doleful cutting tears,
part sting, part shock, and part calculation:
you know it was right and feel quite stricken.

January 16th: Nightsounds

Uhu of the barn owl; cock pheasant's creak;
hackle and cackle; our lyric willow;
and always this ancient house, its whispers
and predictions. One listener: her heart.

January 17th: Dangers

That tinny sound as she tries out thin ice!
In its shine you see capsizes, crashes,
every kind of accident, then, far worse,
the smiling drivers . . . Take steps. And take steps.

January 18th: Joy

Lily, she thought; she thought, *tiger. And this
is my own daughter: dayspring and dancer
and gleam.* The late primrose light faded from
the little room. Still she looked; still she shone.

January 19th: Mother!

The least knock or scratch or ache and you are
supernumerary. Back to the source:
mātr, métēr, mōdor, mutter, máthair . . .
She cries and reaches out. The woman smiles.

January 20th: Dog

Beau Brummel and Barnum and Loyal Sam!
He's her chief barker and mooning paleface,
her game opponent, grinning accomplice.
She tightens the leash: *Jealous! You're jealous!*

January 21st: Imitation

Wading round the room in black stilettos;
intent, loading a pipette; kneading dough,
sleeves rolled up: flatterer in rehearsal,
instinct with longing to learn, to succeed.

January 22nd: Lexicon

*Why not can't I do it? Of course I can.
Slobber-de-bob! Isgusting! There's water
in frogtime. I want to read peoplest books.
I'll run you down. What colour is your talk?*

January 23rd: Sunrise

You left both ladies in the pink, finger-
tips at their temples. Each stone and each leaf
was locked in bristling frost; the whole circuit
of the sky down-pillows and pear-blossom.

January 24th: Rules

Playing percentage is unknown to her.
Draws you wide, kicks the chalk, always ends up
in dock and nettles. Proper anarchist,
years of markings stretched out in front of her.

January 25th: Spring?

Sunlight. Hedgerows and high-wavers all stripped,
all winter-bleached and ready to begin.
The dog waltzes over the fields. She primes
her shining pots with earth and warm gravel.

January 26th: Promises

Her rainbow segments dance; her cardboard clock
with its bold promise pulses. Poor sleeper,
turn, twitch, and twist, whisper of Horrid Things.
Slowly her dove unfurls morning-white wings.

January 27th: Offenders

Her sequinned, squinting elephant exiled
on the landing is the offending book
your devoted grandmother blue-pencilled
and filleted. Each day it grows larger.

January 28th: Proposals

Hot and hectic and armed with a posse
of proposals: *pick-stickers; picklecheese;*
house-of-cards; Humpty; stand-on-my-head . . .
You, niggard, had one and only one: *bed!*

January 29th: There

There it snows. Here it rains quiet always-rain
dropping into your skull. And there the north
and east winds blow. Here the colours hang limp.
There the rose. Here – how sharply you miss her.

January 30th: Commitment

Hide your eyes! She tears across the room, throws
herself on to the Chesterfield, face down,
enters a white shining darkness: no game,
no commitment ever more serious.

January 31st: Goodbye

The world is opening under our feet;
you stoop, sweep her up, you kiss her goodbye.
Three and already a breaker of hearts:
I won't see you ever again, will I?

Do You, or I, or Anyone Know?

It comes up by the roots
                    dangling and unfortunate,
a straggler and victim on the field's margin
never quite caught up in the bruised gold tides.

The air's an intoxicant, laced with the sweetness
of the barley, and clay, and far thunder.

You shake off the chaplet of storm-flies
and, sharp as a bright stoat, bite through
the hempen stalk.
                    You're holding a wand.

A lick of lightning . . .
                    You break off one grain
and tickle it round the cradle of your palm.
It's a kingdom! First you peel away
pale-striped bullseye skin, then plain wrapping.

And now, half-a-minute later, the dark sky-growl.
The storm's still half-a-county off!
                    The smiling cleft;
the ivory sheen; the warm grain still malleable.

You grind it and grit it. Unconvinced
of its relationship to barley-water, you spit it out.

Now the beard: one whisker. You hold the hilt
and run it smoothly between your fingers.
You rub it the wrong way and say, 'It's biting!'

Nothing the eye can see,
                    unlike the storm
gathering and sending shivers through the barley.
Later, you lift my little brass microscope
from its wooden box.
                    How you surprise my childhood!
Properly ginger, you lay the whisker on the glass tray.

I light a kitchen candle – rain-spears and thunder
drive in through the garden gate –
and fiddle with the mirror, the tube, the mirror . . .

Barba dentata: covering one eye with soft fingertips
you level your unblinking gaze.

Cornucopia

for Gillian

Globe

You cradle the globe in your cupped hands.
It is flawed and freckled, and will weep
if you bite it. Circle of dark secrets.

Sustenance

Tawny oats and barley, sinful couch-grass:
the sultry compass nods as you settle
and smile and bare your golden breast.

Plenitude

Orchard of the body, body of the corn,
and in your complete and fourfold garden
moon-faced onions hang on the flaking wall,
wasps crawl over the last of the clover,
the black mulberries hang heavy with blood,
and a buck hare stares at his reflection.

Intentions

In your bright room you brandish a sheaf
of intentions. You're lifting this old house,
with its grey ruff of doves, and shaking it
by the scruff. But in this wink-and-glint
our discussions are decorous as games
of chess. I move caution; I move cash.
Your moves are never only all they seem,
and now you are so many moves ahead.

On Balance

This day belongs to your elder daughter.
Between wild strawberries so late they will
not ripen, and your crumpled pink roses,
she pedalled and balanced for the first time,
not yet four. I saw your grimace and grin –
that fierce unique desire for each of our
children not only to excel but excel us.
I should say this day belongs to you.

Colours

You wear russet and mole and olive;
less often, amber, umber, vermilion.
Yours are the colours of fruition and earth.
Nothing wan or obvious or irresolute.

Here and Now

Little time for the colour of tomorrow,
even less for the cloud of unknowing:
you build your house on the cornerstone
of Now and view with an indifferent eye
the whole condition of uncertainty.

Ledger

But at the equinox you look over your
shoulder. When days mist and the scales tip,
you pull down and dust your faded ledger
and inscribe lances of sunlight (your own
family's occasions) in phrases rapid
and rosy as the leaves on the wild vine.

Toll

Sepulchral clouds and scudding days: your
head's on my shoulder in the lee of the dune,
half-guarded from the wind and whip-and-spike
of the marram. Over the pale strand
the bourdon tolls. The air mauves and quivers.

Studio

A seventh wave, you galleon in and
redistribute everything: flotsam and jetsam
beached by the last tide, already bleached
and curling; the regular bed of nondescripts;
and not concealed but simply overwhelmed,
the precious shapes you're working on,
shining and bold, crucial as blood.
What abundance! So profuse you cannot
be contained, drawing and redrawing lines,
you draw us all into your one design.

Woman

Tap-root; all eyes, breasts and stomach.
Your body's wave breaking, salt and honey.
Sanctus, the angels sing, sanctus, sanctus.
Peace-weaver, pillow-talker, raising
this old house. My five-pointed star,
my point of departure and return.

A Tongue of Flint

I kicked it out of its snug in a mole-hill,
flecked and milky,
                         and listen to it sing
far from home
                how in those same and everyday
acres with their may-hedges and hedges
jewelled with hips, and all those generations
of seething mosquitoes under the oaks,
I sat on the stile
                or stood by the almost
stagnant stream to watch the swift year's wavings.

No breath of wind,
                         nothing but burning cold,
and one old oak dropped half its leaves.
They shaved from limb to limb: a sound near
the edge of sound – the sharpest scraping.

High summer, setting sun. Ten silhouettes,
hefty and black, whisked filthy tails.
                                   They spun,
they wove rose wheels and golden fans.

Then I heard them
                feverish and shrill
and saw the elm quiver. A siege of starlings
singing well above themselves! Two thousand
or ten thousand footnotes and tripping glosses
or the colours of the year.
                         Up, then, up and off
against banks of pearl and grey, shape-changers,
raucous spirits . . .

This tongue, fierce light
has knapped it and east wind stropped it.
I'll pocket it
and go on listening.

Limb

Why this great slop this ashen slake
glimpsed through the blur
should so speak . . .

sleek farms flanking it
Essex–trim
grim Manningtree
across the mud and shaggy spits
like a northern port or frontier town

it's not the sum
not life alongside in despite
and the loyal shore lights shining

when I see the groyne's blackened props
salt–eaten and askew
I wish the water well of them

empty grey ring the sky brightens over
indelicate slosh
its creeks and pulks and oozing banks
all fickle

this is sea's pulsing land–locked limb
the heart's tides' theatre

and look
a loner rises unsatisfied
eager
wrestles with air and reaches and screams

Here, at the Tide's Turning

You close your eyes and see

                        the stillness of
the mullet-nibbled arteries, samphire
on the mudflats almost underwater,
and on the saltmarsh whiskers of couch-grass
twitching, waders roosting, sea-lavender
faded to ashes.

                    In the dark or almost dark
shapes sit on the staithe muttering of plickplack,
and greenshanks, and zos beds;

                                a duck arrives
in a flap, late for a small pond party.

The small yard's creak and groan and lazy rap,
muffled water music.

                  One sky-streamer,
pale and half-frayed, still dreaming of colour.

Water and earth and air quite integral:
all Waterslain one sombre aquarelle.

From the beginning, and last year, this year,
you can think of no year when you have
not sat on this stub of a salt-eaten stanchion.

Dumbfounded by such tracts of marsh and sky –
the void swirled round you and pressed against you –
you've found a mercy in small stones.

This year, next year, you cannot think
of not returning: not to perch in the blue
hour on this blunt jetty, not to wait, as of right,
for the iron hour and the turning of the tide.

You cross the shillying and the shallows
and, stepping on to the marsh, enter
a wilderness.

                    Quick wind works around you.

You are engulfed in a wave of blue flames.

No line that is not clear cut and severe,
nothing baroque or bogus. The voices
of young children rehearsing on the staithe
are lifted from another time.

                              This is
battleground. Dark tide fills the winking pulks,
floods the mud–canyons.

                         This flux, this anchorage.

Here you watch, you write, you tell the tides.

            You walk clean into the possible.

Toll of Winter

So cold the passerines
fold their wings
and do not open them again

the stable bell
that used to tell the quarters
in the shallows of the season
tolled once
told nothing

one fleece on the wold

out damson and russet
and malleable red Welsh gold
in oyster
in pearl in diamond

what earth has it will hold
its seven hundred doors
locked and bolted

Man on mold
thy days are numbered . . .

the blue flames quiver
sleepers curl
and turn to each other
the old grow very old

(and in the margins
the cowled ones wait
the coiled ones
the criers and the splinters

the world's tellers
all keen winter's sounds)

Porlock: Interrupted Lives

Amongst these pink and grey stones,
some smooth, some dressed with ocean runes,
eleven US airmen died;
The salt has almost eaten their names.

The little copper plaque, crammed
by some loving inexperienced hand
(ten men identified and one unknown)
is no longer fastened
tight to the ashen headstone,

and quite soon the stone itself
will crack, or topple
and fall, and for several months
no one will even notice.

A pony down from the moors
nuzzles it; the glistening spoor
of a snail bandages it . . .

Nearby I see what might have been
a little shore sanctuary – a place for prayer
or else a pen for black-faced sheep –
reduced to an oblong shape,
almost no more than a shadow
amongst these dry, quite cordial stones.

I see a mound
and lumps not readily to be explained,
then all around the signs
of other lives and other times.

And where this wilderness is almost bald
I find doomed spears
of samphire irrupting and withering

and a single ragged thistle –
a purple perch
for a butterfly with clouded yellow wings;

and led on by the piping
of a small bird I cannot even see,
come upon a clump of quivering bleached campion.

I stoop and count
the white and shining petals –
ten and eleven and eleven and eleven.

The Signs of Walsham

I have seen the way in. Rightangles and rubber swerves
and deep scummy ditches. I have seen the puzzle on the
palimpsest: the forest of elm and ash, the watering
places.

I have seen the green women, all very elegant and very
particular, trilling in forever light painted in tempera.

I have seen matriarchs who buried their husbands. The
rectitude of pit-props; last survivors. Dispensers of
pullets' eggs and grace-and-favour houses.

Also the old snorters, beady, broad and blunt. I have
seen their terrible horizons.

A woman drifted, she died while spring skipped outside
her window. A newborn baby lolled in the shadow
of the yew tree. I have seen them.

I have seen tides: exiles from collapses and sagging
thatches, shoals of children, the lissom baby-sitters.
Also the old soaks, looking meaningful; buzzing
weekenders; nasal upstarts aspiring to jacuzzis.

I have seen the crusader who lost his name his date and
the crant for poor Mary who lost her heart and died. I
have seen the tradesmen hiding in the wall, the leftover
smiles of oak angels.

I have seen lists of sponsors and meringue-makers,
paragraphs of small type concerning covenants.

Every eighth minute the Bangalore Bomber. The light
plane stoops with its deadly spray. The F1-11s set out
for Libya. I have seen them.

I have seen the kestrel and the tree-creeper; the sun-splash butterflies; the blue sheen on a dragonfly's wings.

The circle of smiles ringing the pink cottages; I have seen it. I have seen slight shoulders, stooping shoulders sharing heavy weather.

Change-ringers stand in the tower. Clay throws up gold. I have seen layer upon layer. And every day this jackwind and its small rearrangements.

Above the Spring Line

in celebration of the Ridgeway

1

Under the moon's pale razor
under the warm eye
under the chamber of clouds
under rain-dance and hail-bounce

in this latitude of shadows

blazing the green limbs
foot-friend and far-reacher
master of compounds

2

Overseer of Epona and the fleet horses at Lambourn
the bigwigs in their hill-stations at Silbury and
  Chequers

keeper of Dragon Hill and the craters on the bombing
  range
also the quaking grass the brome grass melilot and
  eyebright

warden of the Og and the watercress beds and Goring
  Gap
the sarsens like dowdy sheep and the dowdy sheep like
  sarsens

custodian of the downs and brakes the strip lynchets and
  warrens
under the lapwing the glider's wing spring of yellow-
  hammers

3

And spring is the word. I can almost forget
yesterday – the sweat stain semen stain smudge
of chalk and in the hedge the sodden butts
the jagged bottle and a bloodstained rag

Here are wiry snowdrops bedded in beech mast
where wild pigs rooted. Fuses everywhere
The spindle and bryony shrug their shoulders
Birch-twigs pinken, generations within

4

A man laps at a dewpond, lays his hoar-head on his
    knapsack
knobby with Brandon flint. A girl in a mauve shift bares
    her throat
Trials riders tight-lipped burn through crimson and
    purple rosettes

A crocodile of the literal-minded steamy and singing
I will lift up mine eyes set their sights on the escarpment

Ah! the drover sleeps in a butterfly wimple – chalk-hill
    blues
flutter in and out of his mouth and here above the spring
    line
a hunter smiles as he snares such a pretty Chiltern
    gentian

5

It is all within me
written in chalk, and written
in your hand it is yours

whatever you may also choose . . .

From Overton to Ivinghoe
sunlight and ribs of shadow
pressing behind us and coursing
through us. We are conductors

Notes

pp. 11–22: Poems 1, 3, 5, 7 and 9 take details from John
   Constable's (1776–1837) drawings and paintings as
   their starting points. '1 The Happiest Hours': *The
   Cornfield*, National Gallery, London. '3 Creatures of a
   Landscape': *The Mill Stream*, Ipswich Museums and
   Galleries, Suffolk; *Flatford Mill*, Tate Gallery,
   London. '5 Correspondences': *Maria Bicknell*, Tate
   Gallery, London; *Gleaners*, Musée du Louvre, Paris;
   A Church Porch, Tate Gallery, London. '7 Quiet and
   Unquiet': *Boat Building*, Victoria and Albert
   Museum, London; *A Boat Passing a Lock*, Walter
   Morrison Collection, Sudeley Castle,
   Gloucestershire; *A View on the Stour near Dedham*,
   Henry E. Huntington Library and Art Gallery, San
   Marino; *Sketch for Stratford Mill*, Yale Center for
   British Art, Paul Mellon Collection. '9 In Pursuit':
   The White Horse, Frick Collection, New York.

p. 24: The Garden Tent by Thomas Churchyard
   (1798–1865), Tate Gallery, London.

p. 25: The White House at Chelsea by Thomas Girtin
   (1775–1802), Tate Gallery, London.